Adventism's
"Movement of Destiny"

**We Can Be Ready for Impending Events
with Surprise New Meanings
from Old Prophecies!**

This message is so important that everyone should be aware of it and if the reader wants to copy or forward it to share, that's fine. It is the King's servants that bid others to the wedding in Matthew 22 and have their lights burning in Luke 12. We must do so, confident of God's blessing. Thank you for helping!

Richard Ruhling, MD

Total Health Publishing

Contents (Control + click)

"Then shall two be in the field..." "Then" is at the same time, Passover timing, but in the 2nd month.

The Goodman's Broken House This is shown to have the same timing, Passover, 2nd month in Proverbs 7:19,20.

The Evil Servant Smites His Fellow Servants No timing in this parable, but next word is 'then.'

Then shall the kingdom be like 10 virgins Bad translation and overlooked 9/11 clue explained.

Like a man traveling to a far country If Israelites took a long trip and couldn't get back for Passover, they were to keep it the 2nd month-- Numbers 9:10,11.

The Parable of a Fig Tree The barren fig tree represented the Jewish nation then, the US now.

The Wedding Parables Are Not Understood We are asleep with lights out, Matthew 25:5.

The Wedding Feast of Betrothal God got an ignorant bride at Sinai, but "beware the leaven of Pharisees" helps avoid a repeat.

Summary

Appendix: Rx Drugs Are the Leading Cause of Illness & Death Medical Care Is Not Healthcare; It's the #1 Cause of Illness and Death, made so by Adverse Drug Reactions, not an overdose.

Vaccinations and Autism

Education: Taking Your Children Changing policies are a perversion of Bible principles. "You shall teach them..."

Introduction

I'm betting my life that the information I'm sharing here is right and I hope you can follow the Bible's "road less traveled" to discover why I wouldn't trade God's promises for anything else.

The wedding parables are not about a quick snatch to heaven. They are about a covenant relationship with Christ as Israel made with God and He later said, "I am married to you" in Jeremiah 3:14. Doing so also makes us His kingdom, Exodus 19:5,6. This is an external kingdom, not "within you" Lk 17:21.

It's the kingdom that the disciples wanted in Acts 1:6, and Christ's reply linked it to the "times and seasons" that Paul said would come in the end-time "day of the Lord." 1Thess 5:1-3.

"What is has been already; what is to come has been already. God summons each event back in its turn," Eccl 3:15, NEB.

Daniel confirms this: "In the days of these kings shall the God of heaven set up a kingdom…" Daniel 2:44,45. That's not after Babylon falls and no kings are left at the 2nd coming. We have an opportunity that the disciples wanted and it's high reward-- the Bride of Christ gets to share His throne, Revelation 3:21.

So how do we get from lukewarm to sharing His throne? Luke's wedding parable has half a dozen parallels to the above passage, offering us key insights that we consider.

How an Impending Events Will Test Us
Can Christ Save Us If We Don't Do What He Said?

If Christ came in the sky today, everyone would raise their hand and say, "I'm yours—take me!" But it won't happen that way…

Coming events will sort us and readiness to response is the key. Christians cite Christ's knock at the door of our hearts as He is always knocking, wanting to be part of all that we do. This is a nice metaphor, but soon it will apply to an event that's urgent and we "must open unto Him immediately." Luke 12:36.

That's a wedding parable. The wedding parables all show a sudden event, beyond which it's too late to change our destiny.

We want Him to save us, but how can He do so if we don't do what He says? "Many will say, Lord, I did many things in your name and He will say, "I never knew you!" How is it possible?

The word for 'know' is *ginosko,* and it means intimate knowing as in marriage or a covenant. God made a covenant with Israel to prove what was in their hearts, and it wasn't good!

The impending event represented by the 'knock' will test our readiness to "open unto Him immediately." We will explain it later, but for now. For now we want to see how that parable in Luke 12:35-44 has half a dozen parallels to Revelation 3:14-21.

Luke's Wedding Parable for Laodicean Lukewarmness

Laodicea is lukewarm with materialism, but Christ's offer to share His throne (Rev 3:21) is like His promise, "He will make [us] ruler over all that He has" (Luke 12:44) if we meet the conditions that most readers have never considered.

Here are six more similarities in the two passages.

1. Have your loins girded in Luke 12:35 is like the need of white raiment for nakedness in Rev 3:17.
2. Have your lights burning is like eye-salve for our blindness.
3. Both passages have a knock and are to open.
4. Both passages include a meal.
5. "Ruler over all that He has" is like sharing His throne.
6. "When He comes" in Luke's parable is _not_ the 2nd coming in the sky, but as God came invisibly to Egypt to execute judgment and this also fits Ellen White's judgment context in GC 426.

We will look more at Luke's parable later, but the key point for all of the wedding parables is an implied opportunity to be part of the Bride of Christ, 2Corinthians 11:2, but also in the context of "a sudden, unlooked-for calamity," COL 412, 9T 92,93.

The Bride shares the throne and there is a high destiny for the 144,000. Revelation 14:4 says they are virgins—they must be the wise virgins that get into the wedding in Matthew 25:10.

Millerites gave a message, "the Bridegroom comes" as they thought Christ would rapture them to heaven and Evangelicals have also erred re the parables as a misperceived 2nd coming.

The Bible is its own expositor—it explains itself, and we must be like the Bereans to "receive the word with readiness" as we search the Scriptures whether a thing is supported. Act 17:11.

Please look up and maybe mark texts that you aren't familiar with. Sharing with others also helps deepen the impression.

So where's the wedding? It's linked to the greatest event since Creation in the Old Testament—the Exodus! God came Egypt to "execute judgment" (Exod 12:12) and He took Israel to a covenant that made them His kingdom (Exod 19:5,6) and Bride. Jeremiah 3:14 says, "Return, I am married to you!"

God regarded the covenant as a marriage relationship and Paul included the Exodus in "all those things happened to them for examples…ends of the world." 1Corinthians 10:1,11.

Favorite author, Ellen White shows this need in a classic quote: "That which God purposed to do for the world through Israel,

the chosen nation, He will finally accomplish through His church on earth today…even to His covenant-keeping people, …and to them will be fulfilled all the covenant promises made by Jehovah to His ancient people." *Prophets & Kings,* 713,714.

We might wonder how we get from where we are as a General Conference Corporation of churches to a covenant, and that's partly due to our lukewarm blindness in Revelation 3:

The answer comes from another look at the Exodus. We must see that Paul includes the Exodus in "<u>All those things happened to them for examples</u>...ends of the world." 1Cor 10:<u>1</u>,11

This book offers the highest destiny to be part of the 144,000 and they sing the song of Moses, which is a song of a similar experience.

We said the key to high destiny is to "prophesy again" Rev 10:11. That includes a message of judgment similar to 1844. It didn't fit as expected, but we are coming to a <u>time of judgment</u> and everyone deserves a warning of life or death issues <u>as in Daniel 1-6</u>.

The Exodus has lessons for us: "What is to come has been already, and God summons each event back in its turn." Ecclesiastes 3:15, New English Bible

The US is like Egypt--an Exodus May Be Coming!

God "declares the end from the beginning," Isaiah 46:10.

This is the basis for historians saying that history repeats, and God is going to repeat the greatest event of the Old Testament for our time—the end of the world! Here's some parallels.

1. Israel went to Egypt in a time of famine like pioneers came to the New World in a time of famine for the Bread of life because the papacy had forbidden the Bible—people hid it in their homes at the peril of their lives.

2. Egypt was the greatest nation then as the US is now.

3. Joseph saved Egypt in the time of famine. For doing so, Pharaoh blessed Israel and gave them freedom and land, but another king came who didn't know that history and put them in bondage, like pioneers gave us freedom in a Constitution, but leaders now forget it.

4. Egypt killed babies in Exodus 1; the US has aborted 60 million. The US deserves punishment more than Egypt did.

5. Egypt enslaved Israel; the US has enslaved most people in alcohol, tobacco and drugs--we say healthcare but it's bondage. http://LeadingCauseofDeathPrescriptionDrugs.com and we have a rainbow of negative lifestyles.

6. God "executed judgment" on Egypt and took Israel to a covenant that He regarded as a marriage, Jeremiah 3:14.

We need to stretch our minds to see how, but a time of judgment is impending on the US. If Bible prophecy continues right, what's coming will shake the world.

Powerful forces and big money are pushing the US toward global government, but the United Nations is the 'image beast' seen in Revelation 13:14-18. It compels false worship in contrast to US freedoms of the past.

But because of US failure from the days of Roe v Wade and the redefining of marriage by the 'Supreme Court', we are destined to see God making a full end of earthly governments that have spurned His wise laws. He foretold doing so in Jeremiah 30:11,24 and Daniel 2:35,45. Check it if unfamiliar!

Daniel 2 has been verified by 2500 years of history and we look now at Daniel's "vision at the time of the end." Dan 8:17.

SDA Pioneers Got the Wrong Vision at the End!

A Confirming Sign for Us to Avoid Embarrassment

Followers of Baptist preacher Wm Miller, failed to check a concordance. The Hebrew word for "vision" at the time of the end is *chazon*—ram and goat, Dan 8:7, not the *mareh* of 2300 days pointing to 1844 (day for a year in Ezek 4:5,6)

There is more to unpack from this because right understanding is the key to avoid embarrassment like the pioneers had.

13

Since the Medes and Persians in Daniel 8:20 are now Iraq and Iran, this vision is fitting our time and we should wonder, <u>What makes the goat angry to attack the ram</u>?

Ellen White offers insight: "Every prophecy is an explanation of some other [prophecy]" *Education,* 123.

That being so, we find a "day of the Lord" text that's relevant because it's the end-time period and it's the natural extension of "night of the Lord" for calamity and the Exodus (12:41).

It's when nations will be gathered against Jerusalem to battle. The houses will be rifled, the women ravished, half the city goes into captivity…" Zechariah 14:1-3.

With the US Embassy there, it is not hard to see war when it happens, and President Erdogan of Turkey said recently that "Jerusalem is our city." <u>World Israel News</u>, Oct 1, 2020.

Combining "<u>prophesy again</u>" (Rev 10:11) with "the vision at the time of the end" (Dan 8:17) we should do so "when you see Jerusalem compassed with armies…" Lk 21:20.

Ellen White says, "Jerusalem is a representation of what the church will be if it refuses to walk in the light God has given." <u>8T 67</u>. Seeing Jerusalem with armies means impending judgment for the church—spiritual Jerusalem is God's holy mountain (references in Daniel 11:45, Isaiah 11:9) from which the stone is cut for God's kingdom in Daniel 2:44,45.

And since God won't do anything without revealing it, (Amos 3:7) we should try to see how it's revealed. The next verse says "the lion has roared." It's when "the Lord shall roar from Jerusalem…the earth shall shake" Joel 3:16.

That earthquake will cause the Muslims to flee, but the earthquake is likely to impact the San Andreas Fault and trigger the earthquake that Ellen White described for spiritual Jerusalem, citing Zeph 1:8 includes the king's children, 9T 95.

She said, "Buildings great and small were falling to the ground. Many lives were blotted out…It seemed that Judgment day had come." Some readers think the vision was about San Francisco but her citing Zeph 1:8 that God will punish the king's children supports this as Loma Linda. 9Testimonies, 92,93.

Note: "Day of the Lord" for Muslims in Zech 14 and for LLU in Zeph 1:7,8 supports events linked together. They are not just random extracts from the Bible here or there that might happen any time. Zeph 1:8 specifies Passover timing!

Many are looking for "Sunday next" when it's not next and the messenger to Laodicea is needing eye salve!

Titus surrounded Jerusalem at Passover in 70 AD. We may expect similar with a month to "prophesy again" before the earthquake at 2nd Passover as we will see later, but what year?

"Teach us to number our days, that we may apply our hearts unto wisdom," Ps 90:12

#1. Bible scholars agree that there is a 7-year ending that they call the 'tribulation'. This is suggested by the 7 years of famine in Joseph's time, Nebuchadnezzar eating grass for 7 years in Daniel 4, 7 days around Jericho as a type for the fall of Babylon, 7 years that Jacob was betroth to Rachel as a model for our betrothal to Christ. His name changed to Israel; us too?

Those 7 years can't begin just anytime. The Bible has a chiastic structure with paradise at the beginning and end. Man crawled into the chasm of sin in Genesis and crawls out in Revelation.

So when Christ created the world in six days, He rested on the 7th day as the Sabbath, Exodus 20:8-11. The chiastic structure implies He will mediate for 6 years and cease on the 7th year.

For His ceasing to coincide with a sabbatical year, it means that the end-time period of 7 years must begin _after_ a sabbatical year. The next sabbatical is 2022. End-times begin in 2023 (?)

#2 reason for 2023 is that it's 50 years, a jubilee interval from Roe v Wade in 1973. The calamity that fell on Egypt was payback for infant deaths in Exodus 1.

The Exodus was a jubilee event with freedom and the promise of land. The parallel for an impending jubilee 50 years after Roe v Wade begs consideration for 2023.

#3. A breath-taking look--the "day of the Lord" comes in the context of 4 generations in Joel 1:3,4,15. A biblical generation is 40 years, Hebrews 3:9,10. 4 x 40 = 160 years.

The SDA Church organized in 1863. Four generations (160 years) brings us to 2023 when nothing is left of a GC Corp as suggested by the above text, and it also may end our freedom--

Abraham Lincoln issued the Emancipation Proclamation in 1863 and the Civil War brought unity and freedom, but after 4 generations (160 years), nothing is left, vs **4**. This may suggest slavery or a deeper form of bondage.

Like the GC's 10-year or 20-year plan, this is just a working model and will be meaningless if Jerusalem is not compassed with armies at Passover, 2023 (time of judgment, Exod 12:12)

Until then, we should do as Abe Lincoln did, "study and get ready—someday my chance will come."

Support for Exodus II in Ellen White & Bible!

Ellen White offers us a great attitude toward truth when she said late in life, "We have many lessons to learn, and many, many to unlearn." Counsels to Writers, 37.

Sadly the title she chose for her last book was changed by publishers and it obscures an important message. Her titled was *"The Captivity and Restoration of Israel,"* but changed to a meaningless *Prophets & Kings.* Her title is a message in Jer 30:3

"I will bring again the captivity of my people, Israel and Judah, and cause them to return to the land that I have their fathers… though I make a full end of all other nations." (verses 3,11).

Do we want to be in America when the full end is made, or do we want to be part of God's kingdom like Israel became His kingdom by making a covenant on the way to the Promised Land—the land of the covenant, Genesis 15:18.

"Paul tells us, "If you are Christ's, you are Abraham's seed and heirs according to the promise." Galatians 3:29. He included the Exodus in "all those things happen to them for examples… ends of the world," 1Corinthians 10:1,11.

The 1844 message of Judgment fit the Exodus. God said, "I will execute judgment," Exodus 12:12. He also took Israel to a covenant at Sinai, later saying, "I am married to you," Jeremiah 3:14. In 1844, they said, "The Bridegroom comes—both messages will fit soon!

The US is more deserving of Judgment than Egypt that killed babies in Exodus 1--the US has aborted 60 million!

Egypt enslaved Israelites, but the US has enslaved most people in alcohol, tobacco, drugs--some drugs are legal and we call it health care, but prescription drugs make medical care a leading cause of illness and death--this is another form of bondage when God designed the body for self-healing. We can live better by wise choices in what we eat, drink or do, 1Corinthians 10:31. More on healthcare in the Appendix.

Perhaps we could regard the call out of Babylon in Revelation 18 as parallel to the call out of Egypt. Both involve a complete separation from the fallen systems of this world as we see later.

Further support for our own Exodus is seen in 1Thessalonians 5:2,3. "The day of the Lord comes as a thief in the night, for when they shall say 'Peace and safety,' sudden destruction comes on them, <u>as travail on a woman with child</u>."

Egypt travailed with God's first-born, Exodus 4:22. We should look for parallels. Passover was a time of judgment and higher destiny for those who were ready. The wedding parable says, "The Bridegroom comes, go ye OUT to meet Him," Matt 25:6.

Some pastors and Bible students recognize the Rule of 1st Use. Where a word or phrase is first found, it often has a meaning or context to consider for the end-time because Christ is the Word, the Alpha and Omega, the First and the Last," Revelation 1:11. Using this rule, we see examples of how the wedding parables are linked to the Exodus. Here are several examples:

1. The cry at midnight in Matthew 25:6 is first found in Exodus 12:29,30.
2. Having "loins girded" in Luke 12:35 is also first found in Exodus 12:11.
3. "Watching" is found in both Matthew 25:13 and Luke 12:36. It is translated from the Greek word, *gregoreo,* meaning to be awake, that's also found in Exodus 12:10.

<u>Summary</u>: Passover was the time when God executed judgment and took Israel to a marriage covenant at Sinai. Every wedding invitation and every summons to judgment has a date. We have overlooked the links to Passover in the wedding parables and preferred to think we can't know. That's a poor translation of the Greek word, *eido,* which means to be aware or understand.

Christ was telling His disciples that they didn't understand and we will visit this topic later in a look at the wedding messages in the New Testament…

The Appendix article on Ellen White shows why I believe she was inspired. In commenting on the cry at midnight, she likens it to "a sudden, unlooked-for calamity," *Christ's Object Lessons,* 412. This also fits the Rule of 1st Use and points to the cry at midnight in Egypt, Exodus 12:29,30.

This focus on the wedding parables helps us understand why Christ said, "You must prophesy again" after pioneers gave the wedding message, "The Bridegroom comes"--but they were premature, because it's an end-time opportunity we will have.

Therefore, we should understand more of the message to be able to give it at the right time soon. The sequel to "prophesy again" is the judgment in which God will give power to His two witnesses for 1260 days, Revelation 11:1-**6**. See text to confirm.

That's Moses and Elijah power to shut the heavens and turn water to blood--bringing the trumpet plagues, Revelation 8:7,8.

When they finish their testimony, the beast ascends to make war. It will have power 42 months--equal time if we compare Revelation 12:1-7 with Rev 13:5 after the deadly wound heals.

Right now it may seem that God's side is losing in a great controversy between good and evil, but "There will be a series of events revealing that God is master of the situation." Ellen White, _Testimonies for the Church,_ Vol 9, pg 96.

God won't do anything without revealing it by His servants, Amos 3:7, but most people don't bother to see what the next verse reveals! The lion's roar is an earthquake that initiates the end-time "day of the Lord." Christ is the Lion of Judah and when He roars, the earth shall shake, Joel 3:16.

That 'roar' is also His 'knock' because the church where He knocked ended in an earthquake ~63 AD. This is an overview...

Christ's Wedding Parables

Christ's wedding parables are so different that it's easy to misunderstand them or not see what they teach by what they have in common.

For example, they all show a sudden event beyond which one's destiny can't be changed. This will be a problem for those who want to "wait and see" regarding coming events when Christ said to watch and be ready and what we consider here offers enough Bible information to comply.

1. The man without a wedding garment was thrown out in Matthew 22:13. The host provided the garment so the man could have changed in minutes, but it was too late.
2. The women who went to buy oil and came a little late heard, "I know you not…" Matthew 25:12
3. We are to be watching that when He comes and knocks, we may open to Him immediately, Luke 12:36,37.

Another example is the word "watch." Coming from the Greek word, *gregoreo,* it means to be awake. Two of the wedding parables emphasize this--Matthew 25:13 and Luke 12:37…

"Blessed are that servants whom the lord when he comes shall find watching...he shall gird himself and make them sit to eat and come forth and serve them."

That's imagery from the Last Supper on the eve of Passover--and the blessing is based on watching, which also is seen to be protective in three "thief" texts.

1. Christ says, "If you don't watch, I will come on you as a thief," Revelation 3:3
2. "The day of the Lord comes as a thief, for when they say 'Peace and safety,' sudden destruction comes… watch" 1Thessalonians 5:2,3,6. The sudden destruction is likely from an earthquake that initiates the end-time "day of the Lord" as seen in Isaiah 2:12,21. Joel 2:10,11 shows it initiates a series of events, but no 2nd coming!
3. If the goodman had known when the thief was coming, he would have watched and not suffered his house to be broken, Matthew 24:43. Again the broken house, earthquake and coming as a thief are linked, but those who watch may be protected.

Christ's last night was probably a microcosm of end-time events and telling His disciples to watch and pray on the eve of Passover is repeated by Paul to us in 1Thessalonians 5:2-6.

So how should we understand those events? Do we see the lawlessness that is increasing with widespread terrorist acts? It will be coming our way. The evil servant begins to smite his fellow servants, verses 48,49. "_Then_ shall the kingdom …be like ten virgins."

"_Then_" means at the same time or as a direct consequence. The context for judgment in Egypt and the wedding parables support Passover timing. God won't do anything without revealing it," Amos 3:7. "Teach us to number our days that we may apply our hearts unto wisdom," Psalm 90:12 supports a broader focus.

"The Time is Fulfilled" Mark 1:15

When Christ said, "The time is fulfilled," He was referring to the best-known time prophecy in the Bible, Daniel 9:24,25, pointing to the Messiah, a word that means anointed.

But the Jews wanted deliverance from the Romans. They missed the role that Isaiah 53 gives. He came to pay the penalty of our sin and to reconcile us to God. The 70 weeks of years in Daniel 9:24 spanned 490 years with the Messiah coming one week (7 years) before the end of that prophetic period.

Those 70 sevens also spanned 10 jubilees. Jubilee was defined as the 50th year in Leviticus 25:8-10, but the 50th jubilee comes to 1994-95 as explained next…

24

How Papal UN Visits Signal End-Times

God reinforced the weekly cycle of six days to work and the seventh day as a Sabbath that was made for man and it's also the Lord's day, Mark 2:27,28. The yearly cycles were to enforce this concept as Israel rested the land every the 7th year.

After 7 sabbatical cycles (7 x 7 = 49), the 50th year was a Jubilee, but it came every 49 years because the 50th year was the 1st year of the next set of sevens.

In a jubilee year, debts were cancelled and Israelites were given freedom. If land had been sold, it came back to family ownership. A man could not sell his land and impoverish his children permanently. Leviticus 25:9,10.

The 490 years of Daniel 9 spanned 10 jubilees (49 x 10). They began with a jubilee event when Israelites were given freedom to leave Persia to get their land back in 457 BC. (Artaxerxes' decree, Daniel 9:25, Google). The 70 sevens ended in 34 AD--that was also a sabbatical year.

Fast-forward 40 more jubilees from the time of Christ (40 x 49 = 1960 years). Added to 34 AD, the 1960 years bring us to a sabbatical year in 1994 and the 50th jubilee in 1995 when Pope John Paul spoke to the UN <u>on the Day of Atonement</u>. That event fit the timing for Day of Atonement in Leviticus 25:9,10.

Then there was a 20 year gap until Pope Francis' UN visit, also <u>on the Day of Atonement</u> in 2015, but ***why*** <u>a 20-year gap</u>?

Peter says, "Be not ignorant, 1000 years are like a day, a day is like 1000 years…God is not slack...the day of the Lord will come." 2Peter 3:8-10.

If we integrate the jubilees into 1000 years, 10 jubilees of 490 years + 490 more = 980. There are <u>20 years left over</u>, **signaled by the popes' visits at the end**!

This suggests that papal visits at the end of the jubilee timeline marked the end of 1000 or 6000 years when the 7th millennium brings "the day of the Lord"—the end-time period and a time of judgment that Peter says not to ignore, 2Peter 3:7-10.

'When-Then' Signs Marking the End of 6,000 Years

There were also a five 'when-then' signs that marked 2015.

1. "The day of the Lord was signaled by a rare solar eclipse on the equinox. It marked the same time as when God told Moses, "This *chodesh* (new moon crescent) is the beginning of the month, the first month of the year," Exodus 12:2.

If we go to Google images and type *chodesh, we* see it's the thin crescent moon that millions of people understand as the beginning of the new month (not the dark moon on the calendar that no one can see. A "sign" is something we see. Genesis 1:14.

Our Gregorian Calendar has no relationship between the new moon and new month and it is not the focus for when the end-times will begin. The next sign shows when things began for Israel in Egypt...

2. Two weeks after the solar eclipse in 2015, there was a blood moon on Passover. This also is not common, and to have those two events marking the beginning of the biblical year in March, 2015 reminds us that "The sun shall be darkened and the moon turned to blood _before_ the day of the Lord." Joel 2:31.

'Before' is translated from Hebrew, _paniym._ It means facing the "day for the Lord." Those events are facing end-times.

3."The day of the Lord comes as a thief; when they shall say 'Peace and safety,' sudden destruction comes" 1Thessalonians 5:2,3. Iran's Nuclear Treaty in 2015 was 'Peace and safety,' and they have violated it with missile testing.

4. Billy Graham said that God will have to apologize to Sodom if He waits longer to send judgment on the US. The Bible calls homosexuality an abomination in Leviticus 18:22, and it was 'standing where it ought not' (Mark 13:14) in the Supreme Court, adding to the 'when-then' signs like Christ gave about Lot fleeing Sodom, Luke 17:29.

5. Christ warned of the "abomination…standing where it ought not" in Mark 13:14. Early Christians understood His words as meaning Rome and they fled when the Roman army came to Jerusalem in 66 AD. Doing so spared them the siege when Titus returned in 70 AD.

Rome was also "standing where it ought not" when the pope came to the US Congress because our Constitution says that Congress shall make no laws respecting the establishment of religion, but that's what the pope is all about. His *Laudato Si'* is about closing business on Sunday for family values and attending the Eucharist, paragraph 237 of his online pdf.

"Congress shall make no laws respecting the establishment of religion"--the 1st Amendment. Respecting Sunday violates our Constitution and will allow the UN (image beast of Revelation 13:14-18 to compel false worship as the Bible predicts.

Note that Adventists have focused on a poor translation of the above text that says "an image to the beast." There is no Greek word for "to". The Greek says, "make image beast."

A UN New World Order will be the image or look-alike of the Old World Order (papacy) because so many Catholic nations will vote for what the pope wants. Widespread homosexuality and immigration Muslim countries and Catholic countries to the US are examples.

Christ's signs about fleeing Jerusalem may have a parallel for a time to get out of cities? If we do so before a huge event when martial law is set up (Matt 24:40 is like Luke 17:36,37), we can move safely and well. Waiting till we see military means to flee without going into your house to get your things, Matt 24:17,18. The signs as explained above for fleeing justify a move out of cities before big trouble comes.

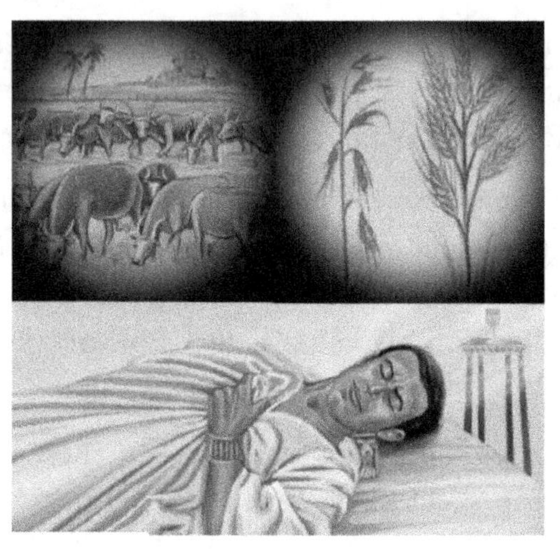

7 Good Years, Then 7 Bad Years, Genesis 41
Trump has been good for the economy

We might wonder where we are in the stream of time. We should be able to know because God won't do anything without revealing it, Amos 3:7.

"Teach us to number our days that we may apply our hearts unto wisdom," Psalm 90:12. God declares the end from the beginning, Isaiah 46:10. In the beginning, Genesis shows how...

Pharaoh dreamed of seven fat cows 'eaten' by seven lean cows and seven full heads of grain ending with seven thin heads. It meant 7 years of famine, supported for us by the king eating grass in Daniel 4--Christ said to understand Daniel in Matt 24.

The book of Revelation integrates historical events into the last seven years. "What is to come has been already, and God summons each event back in its turn," Ecclesiastes 3:15, NEB.

Fat cows and fat heads of grain is the basis for a "Twice Speak" Bible Code that says when something is repeated, it's once for history; the 2nd application is for end-times. Here's why we may be in the seven good years now…

1. There were six days for Creation and then God rested or ceased His work. At the end of 6,000 years we may expect Christ to cease His work of mediation on a 7th year, a Sabbatical year that synchronizes with the Sabbatical year of 2015.
2. Since the bad times haven't begun yet, we are in the 7 good years for the economy that could end with 2022, allowing end-times to begin in the spring of 2023.
3. It's breath-taking to see the end-time 'day of the Lord' comes in the context of 4 generations in Joel 1:3,4,15, and after 4 generations of locusts, nothing left vs 4, NIV. This could mean not much left after four generations of Adventism. A generation is 40 years, Heb 3:9,10.
   The SDA Church incorporated in 1863. Add 160 years and it comes to _2023_, like the end of 7 good years above.

4. The ceasing of Christ's intercession as our High Priest in a sabbatical year fits a 'chiastic' structure of the Bible. The end is a mirror image of the beginning.

Summary: 7 bad years in Daniel 4; 7 bad years in Genesis 41; and 7 days for Jericho like Babylon--6 days with a trumpet each day fit the 6 trumpets in Revelation 8 & 9) and 7 trumpets on the 7th day are like 7 plagues in the 7th year, Revelation 16.

Let's look at more parallels with Egypt…

History Repeats: the US is like Egypt--
Killing Babies and Enslaving its People

Below are five examples of how the US is like Egypt at the time of the Exodus. Proud Egypt was humbled by calamity brought by God. The US is parallel in greatness and pride, but "pride comes before a fall." History and the Bible warn of impending judgment.

Paul said 'the day of the Lord' comes as a thief...when they say 'Peace and safety,' sudden destruction comes on them as travail on a woman with child." 1Thessalonians 5:1-3.

Egypt travailed with God's 1st-born, Exodus 4:22. We should see how the 7 good years in Egypt followed by 7 bad years are also for the US because the US has many parallels to Egypt. Here are five examples…

1. Egypt was the strongest nation then as the US is the strongest nation now.

2. Egypt was the source of food in famine as America is for some nations now.

3. Israel went to Egypt in a time of famine as pioneers came to America in a time of famine for spiritual bread because the papacy banned the Bible—people hid it in their homes at the peril of their lives. They risked their lives at sea or from starvation or Indians, seeking for freedom in the New World..

4. Another king came to power who didn't know Joseph. New pharaohs didn't recognize the rights and freedoms previously granted to Israel.

Like Pharaoh, many in Washington forget the Constitution gives freedom to citizens for self-government, and now federal government is huge, telling everyone what to do or not to do.

The principles of self-government came from the Bible. John Adams, our 2nd U.S. President said "the Constitution was designed only for a moral and religious people." But after generations of TV's sex and violence, we are no longer "a moral and religious people."

5. Egypt killed babies and enslaved Israel. The US has aborted 60 million and has enslaved most of its population with alcohol, tobacco, caffeine and Rx drugs that we call healthcare, but they are a leading cause of illness, disability and death.

People are in bondage to food, fashion, fiction, gambling, greed, 'music,' sex, perversion, TV, movies, violence--a rainbow of negative lifestyles.

We're a nation in bondage by our choices and the Bible shows an impending time of judgment as when God executed judgment on Egypt and took Israel to a covenant agreement that made them His kingdom…

The good news is that God's kingdom is impending. God said, "If you will keep my covenant, you will be to me a kingdom," Exodus 19:5,6.

The only book Christ recommended to understand the end-times says that God will set up a kingdom 'in the days of these kings,' Daniel 2:44. That opportunity for us is impending!

How God's Kingdom Will Be Set Up, Daniel 2

Most pictures of Daniel 2 show a stone coming from the sky as the 2nd coming. But Daniel 2:45 says the stone was cut out of the mountain without hands. What does that mean?

The only other usage of "mountain" in Daniel is Jerusalem-- My holy mountain--it represents God's people, and cut out without hands means no human devising. The GC president has no advantage over members who seek to serve God, who are like the wise virgins in Matthew 25.

Everyone deserves an opportunity to hear and understand what we need to do to be part of God's kingdom for the end-time--

just like in Egypt, there were Egyptians who left Egypt to be part of Israel. They were the "mixed multitude," Exodus 12:38.

When the disciples wanted to know when, Christ linked it to the 'times and seasons' that Paul linked to the 'day of the Lord' (Acts 1:6,7; 1Thess 5:1-3). It includes 'sudden destruction' (earthquake, Isa 2:12,19) as 'travail on a woman with child.'

Egypt travailed with God's 1st-born (Exod 4:22) and we've seen how the US is like Egypt. God is going to judge the US for its sin against great light for abortion and homosexuality. Those who are ready can be part of His kingdom.

Kingdom means dominion of a king. It's about His laws that are in effect "till heaven and earth pass." Matthew 5:18.

We cannot earn our salvation by keeping the law, but we shall not be approved by heaven if we don't want His guidelines.

"If you love Me, keep my commandments." They are not wild ideas--they make good sense and bring us peace, happiness and prosperity. Israel's wisest king, Solomon said, "Righteousness exalts a nation." Proverbs 14:34.

How surprised a heathen spy might have been if he could have crept into Jerusalem's Most Holy Place where the ark was, to discover the secret of Israel's greatness was not a gem-studded idol, but a law—a law that defined our duty to God and others with equality and wisdom for every situation in life!

"The Bridegroom Comes!"

The Bible is God's love letter to us. He wants us to become familiar with it, "here a little, there a little" (Isaiah 28:10) so we see how it fits together before the events happen. God won't do anything without revealing it, Amos 3:7. We need a better understanding to see how the end-times pieces come together.

The wedding parables show different aspects and they seem so different that we miss what they have in common.

Luke's wedding parable is overlooked by most readers, but it is like the Rosetta Stone. The Rosetta Stone was a discovery that helped to understand Egyptian. The hieroglyphics were on a table of stone with the Egyptian and Greek languages. Luke's wedding parable helps us especially with the timing…

Passover is the Time of Judgment and Marriage

Luke's wedding parable has triple <u>Passover imagery</u>, seen below. Also, the cry at midnight in Matt 25:6 and Exod 12:29,30 point to Passover. God won't do anything without revealing it, Amos 3:7, but are we listening?

Passover was the historic time of judgment-- they were to pray for God to pass over them and not let judgment fall on them.

#1. "Have your <u>loins girded</u>." Luke 12:35. That phrase is first found at Passover, Exodus 12: 11

#2. "Watching" (*gregoreo*--be awake) is seen in Exodus 12:10 where Israel ate the Passover and left nothing till morning.

#3. The Last Supper imagery in Luke 12:37 was also on the eve of Passover when Christ girded Himself and served His disciples as He promises to serve us if we are "watching."

Doing so is the key to high destiny, just as a woman's life changes if she marries a king!

The flip side of this is bad news for those who shrug this off. The servant who declines or fails to be watching will be beaten with stripes as Christ said in Luke 12:48.

Rapture thinking says God will not put His bride through tribulation, but the Bible says "we must through much tribulation enter the kingdom," Acts 14:22.

But the plagues fall on those who aren't sealed and haven't made a covenant--"sealed" as seen in Nehemiah 9:38.

The plagues are for those who aren't sealed (Rev 9:4) and who accept the mark of the beast to go along with a New World Order, Revelation 13:14-18; 14:9,10.

But God says, "Behold, I make a covenant (with you)…I will do marvels…I will drive out the Canaanite" Exodus 34:10,11.

We should see a parallel promise in the New Covenant that we may make. God says He will write His laws in our hearts so we want to do the right things. Jeremiah 31:31-33.

Without the New Covenant fulfilled to us, we wouldn't be safe to go to heaven. We might lust after someone or start trouble over again with some issue.

We think not, but we don't even know our own hearts. "The heart is deceitful…desperately wicked," Jeremiah 17:9.

We can see this from Christ's letter to His last church. It's described as 'wretched, miserable, poor, blind and naked,' Revelation 3:17.

Why would Christ want to rapture this group to heaven? We have some growing to do!

God took Israel to the wilderness to prove what was in their hearts, and what they discovered wasn't good. Egypt's history of watching at Passover and two wedding parables support our need to watch at Passover, the historic time of judgment, to be ready, but what does 'watching' mean?

Watching Means a Need to Know When!

Most people think "watch" means to be aware, and everyone thinks they are aware. The Greek word, *gregoreo,* means to be awake and that's how Christ used it in Matthew 26:38-41.

It would be unfair for Christ to tell us to be awake if there were no clues for when, because we can't be awake every night, but Passover was the only night it was commanded.

The wedding parables of Matthew 25 and Luke 12:35-48 offer blessing and high destiny for those who are watching for Christ's coming, so we want to understand what He meant.

James and John wanted to be on His left and right hand in the kingdom. Christ asked if they could drink of His cup, which implies sharing what He would go through.

They said yes. At the Last Supper, He gave them the cup, but hours later when He asked them to watch and pray, they slept.

He said, "Could you not watch one hour?" Matthew 26:38-41. It was the eve of Passover.

SDAs are fond of Ellen White's *"Desire of Ages,"* but we have overlooked her statement supporting Passover…

"As He ate the Passover with His disciples, He instituted in its place the service that was to be the memorial of His great sacrifice." DA 652.2 Isn't that saying we should do His supper in place of eating lamb and bitter herbs?

Christians don't do Passover as Jewish people, but on the other hand, maybe we should eat the Lamb spiritually by reviewing the closing scenes of His life, thanking Him for taking our beating and praying to have more of His Spirit.

We can do this by reading closing chapters in the gospels or *The Desire of Ages,* and if we don't have the book, it's online, https://m.egwwritings.org/en/book/130/info

'Blessed is that servant whom his Lord finds watching when He comes. He will gird himself and make him sit down to eat and will serve him,' Luke 12:37.

They were to "watch and pray" that God would pass over them in any judgment that fell. More on this later…

"Open Unto Him <u>Immediately</u>" Luke 12:36

"Watching" is what Christ is looking for when He knocks. 'Blessed is that servant whom his Lord finds watching--He will gird himself and make him sit down to eat and will serve him, Luke 12:37. who aren't watching, aren't included!

The women who came a little late were not admitted. The man with no wedding garment couldn't change and come back.

"Watching" is protective when "sudden destruction" brings "the day of the Lord", 1Thess 5:2,3,<u>6</u>. It's also when God "shakes the earth mightily," Isaiah 2:12,21, New King James.

That earthquake is the "knock" in Luke 12:36 because the church of Laodicea where Christ knocked (Revelation 3:20) ended in an earthquake circa 63 AD. It may be type & antitype, based on Ellen White's earthquake vision at Loma Linda.

She said "It seemed that…Judgment day had come." 9T 92,93. "Judgment must begin at the house of God," 1Peter 4:17. More information in the Appendix.

43

The Destruction of Jerusalem: a Sign for US

There are wise reasons for this.

1. An estimated 90% Jews in Israel today have no interest in their spiritual heritage. Another 8% are Orthodox Jews who hate Christians. They are there because the UN gave them the land, but it wasn't the UN's land to give. It is God's land and after 50 jubilees--a time when land returns to the original owner (Leviticus 25:9,10) they are about to be chased out.

2. Their return to that land was premature. God said if they walk contrary to Him, that He would punish them 7 times over. Leviticus 26:18,21,28

For 390 years, they went contrary to Him, Ezekiel 4:5. They were taken captive by Assyria in 722 BC. 390 times 7 = 2730 minus 722 BC brings us to 2008, but with no year "0" it was 2009 when they would have been free to return.

But in 2009, Pope Benedict went to Jerusalem and Christ warned believers to flee when they saw the abomination "standing where it ought not," Mark 13:14.

The pope represents abominations and seeing him in Jerusalem on the same year that the exiles could return was a heads up not to return if they understood Christ's warning.

Heeding Christ's warning spared Christians in 70 AD. Heeding His words now would spare Jews if they might reconsider their failure to count the 70 sevens of Daniel 9:24,25 to the Messiah, and the many prophecies He fulfilled, (see the Appendix.)

3. The war that will ensue from Zechariah 14:1,2 will bring an end to Muslim militancy in the Middle East, seen in Daniel 8, which Gabriel said is "at the time of the end." Daniel 8:17.

4. God says He will cause both Israel and Judah to return to the land that He gave their fathers, Jeremiah 30:3. Judah represents Jews who accept the Messiah and Israel represents the 10 tribes that were scattered among the nations and intermarried with Christians that also return, Jeremiah 31:10,16,17.

The reason that Jerusalem is "God's alarm clock" is because when we see Jerusalem "compassed with armies" (Luke 21:20) at Passover (historic timing for Titus' siege) we should expect judgment on the US a month later at 2nd Passover as explained. This would allow a similar time frame for _both_ Israel and Judah to return and come together as dry bones after the shaking (earthquake) and get life as two sticks become one kingdom-- both of these in Ezekiel 37:1-22 after the gathering. Ezek 36:24

A Muslim Ram & President Trump!

In Daniel 8, a militant Muslim ram angers a goat that flies from the west to stomp the ram and break its horns. The horns are said to be the kings of Medes and Persians in Daniel 8:20, but Gabriel said "the vision is at the time of the end," Daniel 8:17. Those areas are now Iraq and Iran.

The vision is half fulfilled with the death of Saddam. The next war is expected to be with Iran. Breaking the horn of Iran ends its militancy. Christians are spared by staying out of the war.

God "declares the end from the beginning." In the book of beginnings, Isaac was spared by sacrificing a ram, Genesis 22:13.

Muslims say Ishmael was the son that was spared by the ram. They celebrate the ram sacrifice each year--it's called Al-Adha.

Muslims should see the Bible is greater than the Quran because as Iran threatens to drive Israel into the sea, the horn (militancy) of Iran will be broken to spare Israel, son of Isaac, spared by the ram sacrifice in Genesis 22:13. They are the ram sacrifice, not Israel (son of Isaac).

<u>Note</u>: Isaac was the father of Jacob whose name was changed to Israel in Genesis 32:28. We might see that Israel was spared when Saddam threatened them. The ram was caught in a **bush** in Genesis 22:13. The breaking of the ram's first horn (Saddam) came during the presidency of George <u>Bush</u>.

We should expect the breaking of the second horn (Iran) during the presidency of Donald Trump because animal horns were used to make trumpets. In Daniel 8:8, the goat that breaks the ram's horn has a great horn (Trump). After the horn of Iran is broken, the goat becomes "great," Daniel 8:8.

This is expected in the 2nd term, suggesting that Trump will win the election in 2020. It's amazing that Trump's campaign-- Make America Great Again—fits the goat that becomes great, Daniel 8:8,17.

Big trouble coming!

Being counted on God's side when troubles begin can spare us 9/11 events. We all know 911 is about trouble. Christ's last six parables have a link to Numbers **9**:10,**11** that provides for when the end-times will begin with Passover timing, but in the 2nd spring month. Knowing this, we can be watching as Christ asked His disciples, Matthew 26:41.

The Flood brought an end to much wickedness and it came with Passover timing (Gen 7:4,11) but in the 2nd spring month as it fit one of Christ's **six** 9/11 clues in Numbers **9**:10,**11**.

We may think that's just an odd coincidence, but to students of Scripture, it's another example of God's infinite mind getting our attention with numbers that all Americans recognize and it implies that another 9/11 is coming!

Noah buried Methuselah, whose name meant, *at his death it will come.* He died as a sign that the Flood was imminent. Noah was unclean for contact with a dead body, Num 9:10,11.

The Flood came with Passover timing, but in the 2nd spring month. Noah entered the ark on the 10th day--that's when the Passover sacrifice was selected in Egypt, Exodus 12:3.

When people refused Noah's invitation, they selected themselves for sacrifice. God isn't arbitrary--He leaves the choice to us.

The good news was a boat--but it didn't seem like good news--they didn't think it would rain-- It takes faith to appreciate God's provision which is usually the focus of *present truth*. Present truth was different for Abraham and Moses.

The prophets called attention to truth for their time but human nature wants it easy--"the old time religion that was good enough..." but we don't realize how much it's changed.

So it is now. There's a time of trouble coming "such as never was" (Daniel 12:1) and we would be wise to consider more of God's provisions to "number our days that we may apply our hearts unto wisdom," Psalm 90:12.

"<u>Then</u> shall two be in the field…" Matt 24:40
Was Christ talking about martial law?

"Then" means at the same time, or as an immediate consequence. The "9/11" timing in Numbers 9:10,11 for Noah's Flood might be ignored if it weren't for "then." But Christ's words got twisted into a fictional series of books and movies that made millions.

The "Left Behind" series was fiction as is seen in the companion passage. When Christ said, "One shall be taken and the other left," the disciples asked, "Where, Lord?"

Christ replied, "Where the body is, there shall the eagles be gathered." Luke 17:37. Christ was not talking about a rapture-- He was referring to the dinner of the birds in Revelation 19:17,18.

Christ's warning might mean martial law and being taken to a FEMA camp. Being taken isn't good. The parallel wording is the Flood that came "and took them all away…"

Being taken could refer to those who don't heed Christ's warning to flee "when you see the abomination" that the early believers understood to mean the Roman army. They fled the city of Jerusalem and were spared the siege by Titus in 70 AD. It was a type of end-times.

The US had a military drill--JADE HELM (**H**omeland **E**radication of **L**ocal **M**ilitants), probably testing how a gun grab might work when the US loses 2nd Amendment rights.

We would also lose 1st Amendment rights if Congress honors *Laudato Si'*, the pope's appeal for Sunday, but Sunday is a religious establishment, and favoring it is against the US Constitution. We need the US Constitution offering equal freedom to all.

The Goodman, if he had known…would have watched and not suffered his house to be broken," Matthew 24:43.

The previous parables are linked to Passover timing in the 2nd spring month "as the days of Noah."

In the 2nd spring month at 2nd Passover, Pope Benedict went to Jerusalem in 2009. He didn't know it was 2nd Passover--it's not something observed by Jews now.

Most Jews have no interest in Moses' laws, nor do Christians, in spite of Christ saying, "Till heaven and earth pass, not one jot or tittle shall pass from the law, till all be fulfilled." Matthew 5:18. But if it wasn't important, why do Christ's last parables all have links pointing to those times?

In Leviticus 23:44 they are called *mo'ed*. The word comes from Genesis 1:14 when God appointed or set times by sun and moon. We don't set times but should recognize how God did so.

Christ is the Lamb, slain from the foundation of the world, Revelation 13:8. Those times foretold when it would happen.

More on this later, but it's significant that Pope Benedict proved to be the goodman in Christ's parable. How so?

The King James Bible only has one reference to the goodman in the Old Testament. It's in Proverbs 7:19,20 where a harlot tells a man, The Goodman is not at home; he is gone a long journey…and will come home at the *yom kece* (full moon).

Passover comes on a full moon, but "long journey" is a clue for 2nd Passover because Israelites didn't travel in winter, and if they took a long trip in spring and couldn't get back for Passover, they were to keep it a month later because of the provision in Numbers **9**:10,**11**.

It is not clear how to understand the full picture. Was Pope Benedict's house (pontificate) broken because he was on a long journey and didn't know when to watch?

Popes are married in a spiritual sense to the church and many Protestants believe his church is represented by the harlot in Revelation 17--so that would also fit Benedict as married to the harlot in Proverbs 7:19,20.

This information isn't against so many fine Catholic Christians who live well and don't know what the leaders and secret societies of their church are doing to take control of America and make the pope head of a UN New World Order, and will move to Jerusalem in the end-times as Daniel 11:45 suggests.

'Then shall the evil servant…smite his fellow servants'

The picture shows Muslim intolerance of Christians, but it fits the papal intolerance to Protestants for centuries as foretold in Daniel 7:25 and Revelation 17:6.

If we think the Vatican is enlightened and tolerant now, Rwanda should jolt us to reality. Nearly a million Protestant Tutsis were slaughtered in spite of so many UN vehicles on the streets of Kigali, that "if you spit, you would hit one."

But the UN was ordered to 'stand down' and let the local (Catholic) government handle it.

John Paul later said 'sorry.' But prophecy for end-times shows many martyrs by guess who?

It could begin with Homeland Security (called Romeland Security by an ex-nun who was raped) rounding up patriot dissidents under martial law. If they favor Bible prophecy over a UN New World Order--global democracy led by the pope, they may not come back from a FEMA camp, Revelation 17:6.

Christ's last night was a microcosm of end-times when He cited Zechariah--"Smite the shepherd and the sheep will be scattered," Matthew 26:31. The religious leaders were smiting Christ--They gave Him to Rome for execution.

"What is to come has been already, and God summons each event back in its turn." Ecclesiastes 3:15, NEB.

There's no 9/11 timing in this last parable of Matthew 24 but the next word is "Then…" It means the same timing as the next parable which again has 9-11 timing, Numbers **9**:10,**11**.)

"<u>Then</u> shall the kingdom…be like 10 virgins"

Five of the 10 going to the wedding arrived too late and could not get in. Let's look closely at the meaning of Christ's words.

He said, "Watch," a clue for Passover as the only night that watching was commanded, Exodus 12:10.

Christ renewed this focus when He said, "Watch with Me-- could you not [be awake] one hour?" Matt 26:38-41. They fell asleep and failing to pray, were unready for events that came suddenly. They scattered as He foretold.

We sometimes think they were stupid, but as a wise Master, Christ chose the best men available. They understood Passover as a likely time of judgment for the things that He was describing in Matthew 24.

But then He said, You don't know… It's a poor translation for the Greek *eido* that means to be aware, consider, understand.

Christ was saying, You don't understand and He explained why--"for [because] the kingdom is like a man traveling to a far country," Matthew 25:13,14.

If Israelites took a long journey in spring and couldn't get back for Passover, they were to keep Passover a month later, as shown again in **9/11** (Numbers **9**-10,**11**).

This is the 5th parable with a 9/11 link. Now comes #6

"For the kingdom…is like a man traveling to a far country." Matthew 25:14

Most casual readers think Christ was merely changing the subject to His last parable and fail to see this 9/11 link because they are unfamiliar with the law that Christ said is in effect "till heaven and earth pass," Matthew 5:18.

Christ's invisible return from a far country, (heaven) to execute judgment in a parallel event as God did in Egypt, will catch most people unready, for the day of the Lord comes as a thief when they say 'Peace and safety.' 1Thess 5:2,3

It comes down to our taking Him at His Word that is clear enough if we have this information in mind. In this last parable, the wise stewards were ready—the lazy servant was unready and he lost the talent that he had been given.

More on readiness later, but one more parable supports end-times to begin in late spring…it's about the fig tree.

"Learn a Parable of a Fig Tree…when Summer is Nigh"

Christ's words in Matthew 24:32 are probably not about Israel replanted since 1947 or 1967, and as said later, most of those Jews now in Israel have no interest in their spiritual heritage.

Christ was probably referring to the fig tree that He cursed a couple days earlier, Matthew 21:19, because it was pretentious.

It was characteristic of the fig tree in that locality to have fruit when it had leaves, but this one, full of leaves, disappointed Christ--it had no fruit.

It was like the Jewish nation then, but it has a lesson for Americans now. Though established as a Christian nation, we are worse than Egypt with 60 million abortions and bondage to substances and negative lifestyles.

And "when summer is nigh" fits 2nd Passover in May when summer is near—not so in April at 1st Passover.

The Wedding Parables Are Not Understood

In Luke's wedding parable, Peter asked, "Is this parable for us, or for all?" Luke 12:41.

In Matthew 22, the King makes a marriage for His Son and sends His servants (this means us) to invite others to the wedding feast, but the invitation is scorned and messengers mistreated until the "remnant" get their city burned in Matthew 22:6,7. (King James Bible)

We might wonder why the invitation to the wedding was scorned, but if we remember the Passover setting, the scorners may prefer cake, steak and milk shake to a feast of unleavened bread at Passover, Leviticus 23:6.

But we should be thinking spiritually. It's not about crackers. Christ said, "Beware the leaven of the Pharisees," meaning their teachings in Matthew 16:12.

Churchmen have leavened the Bread (the Bible) by wanting to make it easy. For example, they say, You don't need to do Passover, but could we consider this…

"As Christ ate the Passover with His disciples, He instituted in its place the service that was to be the memorial of His great sacrifice." *The Desire of Ages,* pg 652.2

Doing the Lord's Supper on the eve of Passover (2nd month for reasons above), and then 'watch and pray' is the perfect way to be ready for end-times to begin as expected by His clues.

To be honest, I tend to fall asleep if I try to "watch and pray" as Christ said, but reading *The Desire of Ages* on the closing scenes of Christ's life and praying between chapters is a great spiritual exercise--it's eating Lamb in a spiritual sense.

"It would be well for us to spend a thoughtful hour each day in contemplation of the life of Christ. We should take it point by point, and let the imagination grasp each scene, especially the closing ones. As we thus dwell upon His great sacrifice for us, our confidence in Him will be more constant, our love will be quickened, and we shall be more deeply imbued with His spirit. If we would be saved at last, we must learn the lesson of penitence and humiliation at the foot of the cross." *Desire of Ages,* 83.4

I don't know anyone who does this each day, but why not an authentic service on the eve of 2nd Passover with time to meditate on what He bore for us?

This is the perfect preparation for Christ's knock in Luke's wedding parable--"[Be] like unto men that wait for their lord, when he will return from the wedding; that when he comes and **_knocks_**, they may open unto him immediately.

"Blessed are those servants, whom the lord when he cometh shall find watching: verily I say unto you, that he shall gird himself, and make them to sit down to meat, and will come forth and serve them." Luke 12:36,37.

We saw earlier that the 'knock' is probably the earthquake that initiates end-times because that's how the church of Laodicea where He knocked, ended, circa 63 AD. And when He knocks (earthquake), we open to Him for the wedding feast.

The Wedding Feast of Betrothal

The wedding feast at Passover is the Feast of Unleavened Bread, but it's not about crackers.

When Christ said to beware the leaven of Pharisees, He referred to their teachings, Matthew 16:12. Church leaders leaven the bread, making it light and easy to swallow without much chewing.

The Feast of Unleavened Bread is different and we need to 'chew' it. It's a 7-day feast (Leviticus 23:6), and it fits the week for Bible weddings in Genesis 29:27.

Those events coincide--they have the same meaning. Communion is union in the Word not leavened, and marriage is union by covenant based on the Word. There are seven topics for 7 days of unleavened bread that have a 7-fold emphasis in the Bible as a mark of end-time truth like the 7's in Revelation.

Here are a couple examples. Christ said before He comes, Elijah "must first come and restore all things." Matthew 17:11.

Elijah comes in the context of the statutes and judgments in Malachi 4:4,5. They have a 7-fold emphasis in Ezekiel 20:11-24 where they are linked to sabbaths as a sign of God's people.

The statutes, judgments and sabbaths are examples of topics to consider for a prenuptial feast of betrothal. Ellen White wrote,

"Christ gave to Moses religious precepts which were to govern everyday life. These statutes were explicitly given to guard the ten commandments. They were not shadowy types to pass away with the death of Christ. They were to be binding upon men in every age as long as time should last." 1BC 1104.6

As the Bride of Christ, we have the role to "restore all things" and if we are faithful to our covenant for 7 years like Jacob was before his marriage, we can eat wedding cake in heaven.

Another example is the supper of betrothal when Rebekah made her decision to marry Isaac. As a miraculous birth and a willing sacrifice, Isaac was a type of Christ and Rebekah was a type of the 144,000, the spiritual bride of Christ that gets to follow Him wherever He goes in eternity, Revelation 14:4.

They are said to be 'virgins'--they must be the wise virgins that get in the wedding in Matthew 25. They are "ruler over all that He has…to whom much is given, much is required." Lk 12:44,48.

For a better understanding of what's required (the 7 topics as the basis of our covenant) the reader is encouraged to get a copy of *The Earthquake & 7 Seals* to consider ahead of time, because they need a deeper look—unleavened bread requires mental chewing.

As Abraham Lincoln said, "I will study and get ready…someday my chance will come." Most people focus on money and what they can trade it for. We must be experts on how "In the time of the end, every divine institution is to be restored." PK 678

"It is more blessed to give than to receive." Acts 20:35. If you've enjoyed this and want to be sure you aren't missing something important please click Donate to select what you'd like to receive at http://TheFallofAmerica.blog God bless you!

Summary

Adventism is a movement of destiny, endorsed by the bitter-belly experience of John in Rev 10:10 when pioneers did everything they could to proclaim a time of impending judgment and the Bridegroom's coming around the world, Aug-Oct, 1844.

To be the movement of destiny now, we must "prophesy again." 'Again' means a 2nd time. Therefore, we have focused on the messages given then and they will fit better now because Gabriel said, 'the vision is at the time of the end," Dan 8:17.

Pioneers saw 1844 as time of the end, but the word for vision in Hebrew is *chazon*—the ram and goat is at the time of the end. So "when you see Jerusalem compassed with [Muslim] armies", we understand the need to do as pioneers did with the messages.

Every Christian deserves to hear the good news of how we can have a high destiny by watching on the eve of 2nd Passover as we've considered. As the king's servants in Matthew 22, we must do as pioneers to bid others to the wedding.

To facilitate sharing, what you have just read is posted at http://TheBridegroomComes.wordpress.com so anyone wanting the information can get it. Please be worthy of the reward by first considering the information carefully and then sharing it.

"To whom much is given…much is required." Lk 12:48 supports a vital role to "restore all things" that are included in a covenant we make in a feast of betrothal—(unleavened bread is teachings). In making a covenant, we become His kingdom, Exod 19:5,6 and He will be our defender, Exod 34:10,11. See also Dan 2:44,35.

Appendix

Rx Drugs Are the Leading Cause of Illness & Death!

cdc.gov/nchs/fastats/leading-causes-of-death.htm

s and
ns

ıs/Immune

ife

:are and
:e

y and Risk

;es and

Data are for the U.S.

Number of deaths for leading causes of death

- Heart disease: 647,457
- Cancer: 599,108
- Accidents (unintentional injuries): 169,936
- Chronic lower respiratory diseases: 160,201
- Stroke (cerebrovascular diseases): 146,383
- Alzheimer's disease: 121,404
- Diabetes: 83,564
- Influenza and pneumonia: 55,672
- Nephritis, nephrotic syndrome, and nephrosis: 50,633
- Intentional self-harm (suicide): 47,173

Can you see anything wrong with the list above? It's a lie!

Adverse Drug Reactions have made medical care a leading cause of illness, disability and death, references below.

The definition of an adverse drug reaction is an unexpected reaction from a medicine "properly prescribed and administered." In other words, it wasn't malpractice. It was a good prescription for that condition, and it was taken as prescribed, not an overdose, but some patients react adversely.

68

Adverse Drug Reactions put 2.2 million people in hospitals and 106,000 died, "making these reactions between the fourth and sixth leading cause of death." *Journal of American Medical Assoc*, 4-15-1998

How many died at home? 199,000 according to the *Western Journal of Medicine*. June, 2000. Deaths in and outside hospitals from Rx totaled **305,000** then, with 8 million admissions to the hospital and 3 million for long-term care (nursing homes--they are messed up for life!)

"From 1998 through 2005, reported serious adverse drug events increased 2.6-fold...fatal adverse drug events increased 2.7-fold." *Archives of Internal Medicine* Sept 10, 2007, p 1752.

But if the 305,000 deaths increased 2.7 fold from 1998 to 2005, it was 824,000 (#1 cause of death) and by 2020 we might expect those deaths to increase 2.7 x 2.7 = 6 million/year, or 2% of the US population—2 out of 100.

Most people aren't close to 100 people, but if you know 50 and 1 of them dies, you figure the doctor did the best he could, no big deal. We are numb to figures and awed by the news and want to believe that new drug will cure my problem.

Confronted with medical literature of Rx drugs as the #1 cause of death, a U.S. senator said I was wasting my time, "they own us," referring to the pharmaceutical industry that spends millions per year on congressional re-election campaigns.

Marcia Angell, MD, former editor of *New England Journal of Medicine,* now teaching at Harvard, wrote "The Truth About the Drug Companies, How They Deceive Us".

Robert F. Kennedy, Jr. understands this. He says the vaccine has captured the Center for Disease Control and the UN's World Health Organization. All of the 72 vaccines mandated for children are produced by four companies: Merck, Sanofi, Pfizer, and Glaxo-Smith Kline. No vaccine ever has been safety tested with a real placebo. He says the CDC functions as a vaccine company with a budget of $11- billion per year. $5-billion is spent on buying vaccines at inflated prices. The CDC approves vaccines, buys them from their manufacturer friends, and then forces 78-million people to use them even though they have never been tested for safety. In addition to making $60-billion per year selling vaccines, the companies make an additional $500-billion selling medications for diseases the vaccines cause. ttps://needtoknow.news/2020/02/robert-f-kennedy-jr-on-the-stunning-corruption-in-the-vaccine-industry-that-has-killed-hundreds-of-thousands-of-americans/

My wife, Norma, was in good health and as a chiropractor's daughter, she didn't believe in prescription drugs, but she got a bladder infection.

She got a prescription for Cipro, often used for urinary infections. Norma was better after only 2-3 days when she discontinued it. But a few months later she developed a rash due to petechial hemorrhage. I suggested she see her doctor. He called back after a blood test to say he made an appointment for her the next morning at a hematologist.

Long story short, her blood platelets that were supposed to be 100,000-200,000 were 20,000. Over the months that followed, she had a splenectomy and high doses of Prednisone, blood transfusions and gamma globulin.

Her platelets continued to drop and she developed a severe headache one evening and I had to help her back from the bathroom. She died of a stroke (brain hemorrhage.)

Her doctor signed the death certificate as Idiopathic Thrombocytopenic Purpura.

But "idiopathic" can also mean idiotic on the part of the doctor for not knowing the cause, and pathetic on the part of the patient; that's "idiopathic" (unknown cause).

Looking up Norma's antibiotic—the only Rx medication she had taken during our 19 years of marriage, I discovered that Cipro (taken a few months before her trouble began) can affect the bone marrow and cause the platelet problem she had.

I agree with Dr. Carson that Obamacare, which forces medical care on people who may not want prescriptions or vaccinations, "is the worst thing since slavery."

It is interesting that in the Bible, Revelation 18:2-4 makes a call to come out of the confused systems that it calls Babylon: "be not partakers of her sins that you receive not of her plagues …for by her <u>sorceries</u> were all nations deceived," verse 24, but the Greek word is *pharmakeia*.

I believe true physicians should be seeking an understanding of natural remedies, particularly how a vegan diet can reverse most diseases as seen on YouTube. Search names of Drs. Amen, Neal Barnard, Colin Campbell, Esselstyn, Joel Fuhrman, M. Greger.

Sorcery may seem like a harsh word, but when a person takes a chemical that the body sees as a poison, yet relieves the symptoms, it seems like magic or sorcery, but trouble comes sooner or later.

Drill's Textbook of Pharmacology in Medicine, Chapter 5, Mechanisms of Drug Action, offers this classic quote:

"Drug action always represents artificial interference with the natural functioning of the organism. In the widest sense of the word, every drug is by definition a poison. Pharmacology and toxicology are one, and the art of medicine is to use these poisons beneficially."

It would be better to eat less grease or fried foods, less salt, less alcohol and caffeine, getting exercise and sleep to neutralize stress. All of these are choices that reverse high blood pressure and are taught in the NEW START evangelism series offered to churches later. Please give it a look!

Another example of how medical practice is poison, is the use of mercury as a preservative in multi-dose vials of vaccine. They say the amount is small, but if they warn pregnant women not to eat tuna fish because of the mercury content, why do we inject it into tiny infants?

The symptoms of autism & mercury toxicity are the same: loss of speech, social withdrawal, reduced eye contact, repetitive behavior, hand-flapping, toe-walking, temper tantrums, sleep disturbances and seizures.

By 2 months of age, a baby gets a 2nd dose of Hepatitis B vaccine and SIX other shots--a total of 8, when their tiny systems cannot handle the mercury.

https://kidshealth.org/en/parents/med13m.html The result?

Japan has a much lower incidence of autism--they delay the vaccination process till after 1 year of age when the baby's immune system is more developed.

Why vaccinate? I reared six children with no vaccinations and they all grew up healthy. Mennonites and others that don't vaccinate have no autism. Here's a powerful 1-minute video on autism by pediatrician, Dr Mayer Eisenstein says, "No vaccinations, no autism!" https://bit.ly/2knnIKI

At the time of this writing, Korea reports 48 dead from covid vaccination! Need to Know News

The information on drugs and mercury fits well with what Ellen White, a favorite author wrote 100 years ago--

"A practice that is laying the foundation of a vast amount of disease and of even more serious evils is the free use of poisonous drugs. When attacked by disease, many will not take the trouble to search out the cause of their illness. Their chief anxiety is to rid themselves of pain and inconvenience. So they resort to patent nostrums, of whose real properties they know little, or they apply to a physician for some remedy to counteract the result of their misdoing, but with no thought of making a change in their unhealthful habits. If immediate benefit is not realized, another medicine is tried, and then another. Thus the evil continues.

"People need to be taught that drugs do not cure disease. It is true that they sometimes afford present relief, and the patient appears to recover as the result of their use; this is because nature has sufficient vital force to expel the poison and to correct the conditions that caused the disease. Health is recovered in spite of the drug. But in most cases <u>the drug only changes*</u> the form and location of the disease. [*<u>This describes Adverse Drug Reactions!</u>]

"By the use of poisonous drugs, many bring upon themselves lifelong illness, and many lives are lost that might be saved by the use of natural methods of healing.

"The only hope of better things is in the education of the people in right principles. Let physicians teach the people that restorative power is not in drugs, but in nature. Disease is an effort of nature to free the system from conditions that result from a violation of the laws of health. In case of sickness, the cause should be ascertained. Unhealthful conditions should be changed, wrong habits corrected. Then nature is to be assisted in her effort to expel impurities and to reestablish right conditions in the system." *Ministry of Healing,* p 126,127.

Ellen White's inspiration to have a school to teach natural remedies was a century ahead of our times, and it's sad that church leaders did not respect her "no" to the teaching of pharmacology. They wanted Loma Linda to be accredited by the American Medical Assoc. Against her will, they voted it and became like other medical schools when they had light pointing to something better.

The smartest people went to Battle Creek Hospital for natural treatment without drugs a century ago--these included people like Wm Jennings Bryan, Luther Burbank, Admiral Byrd, Dale Carnegie, Amelia Earhart, Thomas Edison, Henry Ford, etc.

Reader: If you would like a Sabbath program at your church to focus on health and natural remedies, email Ruhling7@juno.com A Blue Cross manager said it's the best he had seen in wellness.

Education: Taking Your Children

Since kicking God out of the classrooms, the educational system has been getting worse with each decade.

Parents naturally want the best for their children. It's an instinct, and it's a biblical thing.

If we take care of our children when they are small, they can reciprocate when we are old and need some help.

Rarely does a child have to do more for his parents than what they did for him growing up.

This is a biblical form of Social Security and it worked well in Bible times, but things change.

The government has intruded into the family circle and claims the right to take your child and teach what you don't believe is right, including sex education and perversion.

At the time of this writing, the state of Illinois is mandating LGBT education (Lesbian, Gay, Bisexual, Transgender). This is an abomination that causes the land to spew us out. Leviticus 18:22,25

If you love your children, get them out of the public schools that are doing so poorly. So much of what they say is education is not needed for life or work.

Having had 25 years of training to become board-certified in Internal Medicine and to teach on the university level, I would say that 90% of what I learned in college or medical school was not necessary.

That includes a chemistry major in college, calculus, physics, zoology, English literature, political science, history.

Medical school was similar with a focus on anatomy, biochemistry and other topics that are mostly forgotten by graduation. We lose what we don't use.

Why not a system of apprenticeship under a competent person instead of book learning?

Another hazard of public schools now is the requirement of vaccinations and shots that are risky to one's health.

The Bible says, "Thou shalt teach them." Deuteronomy 6:7. That's how Christ learned. "The schools of His time He did not seek…" (Ellen White)

Bad Government

When Christ said, Render to Caesar the things that are Caesar's, and to God the things that are God's, He separated the first table of the Ten Commandments with duty to God from the second table--duty to our fellowman.

The First Amendment of the Constitution says, "Congress shall make no laws respecting the establishment of religion." But the statutes of the Bible were guidelines that protected the Ten Commandments and government should make laws that protect the second table of the Decalogue.

But from the days of Roe v Wade, approval of abortion and homosexuality and the opening of our southern border to millions coming for housing, food stamps, education and medical care at tax-payers expense, our nation has gone down.

Congress loves drug company gifts that "blinds the eyes of the wise and perverts the words of the righteous," Exodus 23:8.

79

It's no wonder that Congress was eager to approve 20,000 pages of the 'Affordable Care Act' (Obamacare), written mostly by the drug companies. As Dr. Ben Carson said, It's the worst thing since slavery.

The FDA fails to regulate drugs as they accept money from drug companies and they were soft on Monsanto that now pays billions for cancer victims of Roundup.

GMOs are another problem. Most legislators are sold out and America is going down.

This might also be understood from the CDC owning patents on vaccines so there are mixed motives for them telling us that we need to vaccinate our children--<u>click</u> for previous comment.

9/11 is another example. 1000 engineers have signed a document that jet fuel could not melt the steel beams of the World Trade Center.

What should we think of Defense Secretary, Donald Rumsfeld announcing $3.4 <u>Trillion</u> lost in the Pentagon budget the night before 9-11?

It never made headlines the next day--a missile (plane?) hit the accounting dept, no follow up could be done! If we think this was done by Muslims trained on small planes in Florida, we could be badly deceived.

Leaving Babylon…the Cities

From the days of Lot in Sodom to the present, cities have been a focus of crime and immorality.

Cain, the first murderer, built the first city. Their primary lure is easier work. Men left the farms for a 9-5 job but it's been downhill since then.

It's a false economy as the agricultural base of support has shrunk and fewer people are able to raise their own food.

Millions now flock to the cities for welfare and housing. Government is bankrupt for answers. Cities are considered to be 'deathtraps' by some. Joel Skousen's *Strategic Relocation* is about survival in areas of low population density. All of this fits the Bible message, Babylon is fallen, come out…

If We Fight, We Die in the Coming Civil War

Godly men fought for this country and braved death to establish its freedom in 1776.

But the clock can't be turned back to 1776. We hate what we see happening to America–there's been too much "change."

Colonel Ammerman, under General Schwarzkopf in Desert Storm, cited unclassified information to say there were a million UN troops in North America, mostly on closed military bases (maybe two decades ago, so we might double it).

<u>Department of Defense Confirms Russian Troops To Train On U.S. Soil.</u> Although this is the first time Russian troops will train on U.S. soil, soldiers from other nations have done so for decades.

Perhaps this is because they won't hesitate to shoot US citizens in situations where US troops have concern for the Constitution, (already with a high suicide rate) and might have a problem doing so.

"History repeats" and the following parallel should be instructive to us. When Israel failed to honor God as America has, God allowed the Babylonians to take them captive.

Ellen White saw "War, bloodshed, privation, want, famine, and pestilence were abroad in the land." *1 Testimonies, 268*.

We must not engage in war. Jeremiah said, _If you resist, you will die,_ "but he that goes out and falls [surrenders] to the Chaldeans that besiege you, he shall live." Jeremiah 21:9.

Paul included the Exodus in "All those things happened for examples… ends of the world," 1Corinthians 10:1,11.

"If you are Christ's, you are Abraham's seed and heirs according to the promise [of land]" Galatians 3:29. When New World Order is set up and you can't buy or sell without being compelled to worship falsely (Revelation 13:15-17), the land of the covenant that God made with Abraham will be the only place for true Christians.

It's also the focus of Ellen White's last title, "The Captivity & Restoration of Israel," changed by publishers to Prophets & Kings. Sadly we miss her message based on Jeremiah 30:3 that God will bring again His people to the land of the covenant.

Going there is also the context of the New Covenant Promise to write His laws in our hearts, Jeremiah 31:8,10,17,31. We must have this experience in order to meet Christ in the sky.

It's an awesome thought. That's the last place we might like to go now, but after Zechariah 14:1-3 God will fight against those nations, it will be safe to go, it's also promised in Ezekiel.

"I will take you from among the heathen (America is getting that way!) and gather you out of all countries and will bring you into your own land. THEN (we get a new heart and right spirit without which we will not be ready to meet Christ in the sky)…and you will dwell in the land that I gave your fathers." Ezekiel 36:24-28 (t's not about America anymore!)

We might not want to go there, but there really isn't any choice if we want to be biblical Christians--it's the land of the covenant, promised by God to Abraham's seed, and "If ye be Christ's, then are ye Abraham's seed and heirs according to the promise [of land]" Galatians 3:29.

When the whole world is under New World Order and can't buy or sell without false worship (Revelation 13:15-17) they will receive the wrath of God, Revelation 14:9,10--then God will defend His covenant-keeping people in the land of the covenant–Exodus 34:10,11. Paul said, 'All those things happened to them for our examples …end of the world, 1Corinthians 10:1,11.

84

Roots and How History Repeats

The Founding Fathers understood many of the biblical principles we've mentioned, and they wisely crafted a constitution that maximized freedom of individuals while minimizing the power of government.

But as President John Adams said, "Our Constitution was made only for a moral and religious people. It is wholly inadequate to the government of any other."

Many early Americans understood that the sea beast in Revelation 13:1-10 was the papacy that they had fled. Its 'deadly wound' was the Protestant Reformation, and now that wound is healed as foretold, seen by Lutherans having joint communion with Catholics to end 500 years of division.

A friend asked a Mexican couple why they moved to Montana. They replied, "Because the priest told us to…" Catholics have strategized to outmaneuver other voting blocks in gaining control of most local governments.

"When the time comes and men realize that the social edifice must be rebuilt according to eternal standards, be it tomorrow, or be it centuries from now, the Catholics will arrange things to suit said standards.

"They will make obligatory the religious observance of Sunday on behalf of the whole of society and for its own good, revoking the right of free-thinkers and Jews to celebrate incognito, Monday or Saturday on their own account. Those whom this may annoy, will have to put up with the annoyance.

"Respect will not be refused to the Creator nor repose denied to the creature simply for the sake of humoring certain maniacs, whose frenetic condition causes them stupidly and insolently to block the will of a whole people." *The Liberal Illusion,* Louis Veuillot, published by the National Catholic Welfare Conference, Washington DC.

Rome admits that there is no biblical authority for Sunday worship—it is on the basis of their church authority. This will bring "Protestants" to a test of their "Sola Scriptura" that they claim is the basis of their faith.

When the US accepts UN sovereignty, the pope will get his 42 months as foretold in Revelation 13:5, and it will be time for the 3rd angel's message when it will have an effect that it cannot have now, *Great Controversy,* 606. For further support, "The Godfathers" by Chick Publ. by a converted Jesuit is good.

Singles: Finding the Right Person to Marry

This is a short different focus from what we've been considering, but there are lots of people for whom this information could help.

A young couple asked a pastor to marry them, but the girl's parents did not want them to marry. They said he was not right for their daughter. They appealed to the pastor for help.

He met with the couple and said he would marry them if they would spend a week talking about anything they wanted to talk about each evening, but no hugging or kissing.

A couple days later the girl called to say, 'He is the biggest bore I've ever met!' The wedding was off. She had been misled by affection that human nature likes.

87

Too many think they love each other because of physical affection, but that should only be the frosting on the cake of a good relationship that communicates well with each other.

Focus on the Family said 1st century marriages were contracted when a man and his son would visit another home of a man and his daughter.

The men would talk about the dowry price and the couple might be talking for the first time. They probably talked about everything--work, family, money, sex, religion, children, etc.

If the conversations were both agreeable, the father would give his son a cup of grape juice. He would offer it to the young lady saying, "This is my blood--I would shed it for you." If she accepted and drank from the cup, they were officially engaged.

He went home to build a room on his father's house and she would sew and get ready for his return in a year for the wedding.

The key to happiness involves a mutual asking of wise questions and honesty in answering, but it was not clouded by physical affection that often misleads people today.

Sex may be the frosting on the cake of a good relationship, but many people only have frosting and soon they get sick…

Men play at love to get sex and women play at sex to get love. In the end, the woman loses, but truthfully, they both lose.

After my wife died from a prescription (explained in the chapter on health) I joined a Christian Singles Dating site. Those that I talked to wanted me to move nearby to get acquainted.

Moving was costly and risky if she wasn't the right person, so I asked them, Do you want a biblical marriage?

After explaining the information on 1st century marriages, most weren't so sure. Several wanted the "dating" process. But one woman was brave enough to talk the issues and we had lots in common that included food allergies--I'm blessed with a loving wife who's an excellent cook of foods that I can eat and it's been happy for ten years plus.

As a further help to singles, it is usually the man's role to initiate things, and a woman should not dress in a way that is tempting to lustful thoughts.

Neat and clean with modesty is a biblical principle, and not forward. On the other hand, Naomi's counsel to Ruth re Boaz seems forward but we don't know the customs then.

If single, pray and ask God to lead. The wives of Isaac, Jacob and Moses came from the well--they were taking care of sheep.

Christ said, feed my sheep. Finding someone else with a similar interest in spiritual things is reassuring.

The Stone Kingdom as Bride of Christ in Daniel 2

1. "In the days of these kings" Dan 2:44. The 2nd coming in Rev 19 is _after_ 7 plagues when no kings are standing in Rev 16,18.

2. "shall the God of heaven set up a kingdom." Dan 2:44. This is not at the 2nd coming for a pre-millennial reign on earth. It's like God did in Ex 19:5,6 after judgment on Egypt. 1Cor 10:_1_,11

3. The stone is cut out of a mountain, Dan 2:45. The only other usage of 'mountain' in Daniel is Jerusalem, God's 'holy mountain.' Dan 9:16,20, 11:45 refers to His people. "Jerusalem is a representation of…the church" 8T 67.

4. The stone is cut out "without hand" Dan 2:45. No human devising. GC officers have no advantage over those who study God's Word to obey it.

5. <u>Times and seasons</u>* in Dan 2:21 was Christ's reply when the disciples wanted to know when the kingdom would be restored, Acts 1:6. Paul said we know <u>them</u>* "for the day of the Lord [the end-times] comes as a thief with sudden destruction...as <u>travail</u> on a woman with child." 1Thess 5:1-3.

The Bride of Christ will vindicate God's law when the devil says it can't be kept. The 144,000 who "prophesy again" with understanding will be ready for the judgment in the next verse. They are given power to shut the heaven and turn water to blood (like smashing the image's kingdoms to powder in Dan 2:35)

The Greatest Woman in History–Ellen White?

Ellen White founded a church with counsels to establish schools, health institutions and publishing houses that now belt the world. The most translated woman ever, she overcame obstacles to write 50 books–10 classics on health, education and commentary of the Bible that can be read freely online at **http://www.whiteestate.org/books/books.asp**

She did all of this with little formal education and while facing church leaders who opposed her, asking her to go to Australia, voting a **Catholic church structure**, to which she responded, "How is the faithful city become a harlot? My Father's house is made a house of merchandise, a place whence the divine presences and glory have departed." 8 *Testimonies,* 250.

Two years later she said the apostasy would continue till the Lord comes. Special Testimonies, Series B, #7.

BT Anderson, retired custodian said that leaders burned Series B in the basement of former GC building. She said the burning of Jeremiah's scroll was "a record of historical events that would be repeated …to receive warning, read carefully." 4BC 1159. She said, "We cannot now enter into any new organization" 2SM 390 (1905) but it's where we are now since the GC re-incorporated in 1904.

Like Israel, God chose a weak woman whose childhood injury ended her formal education at age 9, yet her life was huge with all of the above accomplishments that she credited God for.

When she died, she left behind 25 million written words, a total literary output of 100,000 printed pages. In 2015, her book, *Steps to Christ, was available in* **165 languages.**

Dr. Clive McCay, Professor of Nutrition at Cornell University reviewed Ellen White's writings on health and nutrition. He was surprised that she did not incorporate the fads and fallacies of her time and he summarized a **six-page review** by saying,

"In spite of the fact that the works of Mrs. White were written long before the advent of modern scientific nutrition, no better over-all guide is available today."

Ellen White encouraged the purchase of a property in Loma Linda, California that she said God had shown her, but when the day came, leaders had no money for the $5000 deposit until the mail arrived with a letter from Ellen White mailed a month earlier from New Jersey with a $5000 check for the deposit!

Her vision for the school was to train gospel workers to go house to house, singing gospel songs, giving Bible readings and instructions on eating, along with natural remedies and treatments that she said God would bless in answer to prayer.

Today this sounds like weak medicine, but this author's father, a graduate of Loma Linda and who later taught at St. Louis University said 65 years ago that 85% of his patients would get well no matter what he did; 10% he helped and 5% would die no matter what he did.

If we applied those figures to Ellen White's plan for natural treatments and instructions on eating, 95% of people would get well with no need to see a doctor for another prescription. Ellen White did not want pharmacology taught at Loma Linda, but leaders, eager for AMA approval, gave in to pressure to be recognized, and now prescription drugs are a leading cause of illness and death due to adverse drug reactions.

Her book **_Education_ was eulogized** by Florence Stratemeyer, Professor of Education at Columbia University and a leading educator—"The breadth and depth of its philosophy amazed me. Its concepts of balanced education, harmonious development, and of thinking and acting on principle are advanced educational concepts, the teaching of parental responsibility, and the emphasis on self-control in the child are ideals that the world desperately needs.

"Mrs. White did not necessarily use current terms. In fact, she did not use the word *curriculum* in her writing. But the book **Education** in certain parts treats of important curriculum principles. She was concerned with the whole learner—the harmonious development of mental, physical, and spiritual powers.

"Today many are stressing the development of the intellect. But feelings and emotional development are equally important. In our changing society, the ability to act on thought and in terms of principle is central. It is this harmonious development that is so greatly needed, yet so generally neglected today.

It's an excellent help in home-schooling and everyone familiar with what's happening in US schools should be considering what the Bible says—"You shall teach them..." Deuteronomy 6:7. A current headline says, Schools Approve Teaching Students: **'It's Okay To Break The Law, Police Are Evil'**

Just as Adventist leaders made a huge mistake by seeking AMA accreditation for their health work, they did the same in seeking accreditation for their schools. Now when it's clear that the world is ignorant of true education, Adventism has little to offer when it could have been "the head and not the tail" (Moses' blessing if the Jews did Deuteronomy.)

IF THE CHURCH HAD FOLLOWED ELLEN WHTE'S COUNSELS ON EDUCATION & HEALTHCARE, SDAS WOULD BE "THE LIGHT OF THE WORLD" TODAY

Some have tried to undercut Ellen White with accusations of plagiarism, but the statements by McCay and Stratemeyer above disprove it. At worst, she was an inspired borrower who knew what was true.

Attorney Vincent Ramik, a Roman *Catholic*, spent more than 300 hours researching *Ellen White* to say she was not a plagiarist and her work did not constitute **copyright infringement.**

It was her godly counsels written in about 50 books that include *Testimonies for the Church* in nine volumes, that made a huge difference for Adventism. Other 7th-day churches starting in the mid-1800's like the Church of God (Seventh-day), for example in 2012 had ~ 200,000 members and 7th-day Baptists about half as many, but 7th-day Adventists have over 18 million members worldwide with churches, schools and hospitals exceeding every other Protestant Church.

Her vision of 9-11, published in 1909 is **in Vol 9, pg 11-13** of *Testimonies for the Church.*

 A measurement of a person is not only what they wrote, but obstacles they overcame. She faced opposition from church leaders that rejected the 1888 message of righteousness by faith. She went to campmeetings with the proponents (two brilliant ministers) until church leaders wanted her to stop and asked her to go to Australia to start a school. She submitted and from Australia wrote some of her best books.

Background & Perspectives

There was a time when I thought people who left the church were like people who fell off the path--the devil got them somehow--maybe a bad habit or sin they hadn't overcome, but I now see it differently.

As a youth of 14, I experienced God's power in helping me sell Bible story books for children and I was a student missionary to Columbia and Venezuela in college. I was leader of the Medical Evangelism Seminar as a medical student--we studied God's plan for Loma Linda, and when a mission opportunity didn't work out, I was invited to take further training and teach.

At each step, I sensed God's leading in my life and I'm not bitter. 33 years ago, I attended a prophecy conference and heard topics never discussed in Bible or Sabbath School classes.

I began to see a disparity between what the church says or knows and Ellen White's attitude of openness for more truth.

I believe, when considering her obstacles in life and what she accomplished, very few men have lived better than Ellen White.

She supported topics that we don't hear about in church. We should wonder why Elijah is going to come to "restore all things" (Matt 17:11) if we already have it?

Maybe the "little horn" of Daniel 7:25 got rid of more than we know if the papacy in Revelation 17 is the "Mother of Abominations" (verse 5).

We might wonder how the SDA logo of three angels became three squiggles. The words in fine print on the "SDA" logo (previous page) link it to the Jesuits, founded by Ignatius Loyola.

It's been 70+ years since BG Wilkinson, President of Washington Missionary College discovered a Jesuit in his Bible department and fired him. Since then no Jesuits have been found or fired.

Alberto Rivera, a converted Jesuit priest says Adventism is infiltrated as heavily as any church. His wife said he was poisoned for exposing Rome in numerous booklets published by Jack Chick (Chick Publications) like *The Godfathers,* (the Vatican role in WWI & WWII), *The Betrayal* (Lincoln's assassination) and *The Prophet* (how Muhammad got Catholic mentoring via his wife, Khadijah, from her Catholic uncle so that Fatima, Mary and use of force are found in both religions.

Jack Chick described Catholicism as follows:

Rome in a position of weakness is gentle as a lamb.
Rome in a position of equality is clever as a fox.
Rome in a position of strength is fierce as a tiger.

We've seen gentleness and a clever fox. We are about to see the terror of a tiger, but before it comes, God wants a warning to be given.

This is _**not**_ about the Investigative Judgment that the Bible endorses as "the time of the dead that they should be judged" in Revelation 11:18.

It's about the judgment of the living--life or death issues as in Daniel 1-6. Christ said to read and understand Daniel and in the same verse, He said to flee when you see "the abomination… standing where it ought not" in Mark 13:14.

1ˢᵗ Angel: Judgment & Sudden Persecution?

30 years ago at a prophecy conference in Denver, Elmer Johnson of Boulder gave this author a page with a "lost vision" of Ellen White as recorded by Will Ross and confirmed by Elder Robinson. See and consider it now:

https://bit.ly/2V5WFBd

This author heard a trucker 20 years ago say on radio that he took a load to a Catholic Church in Nebraska and he was told to come back in two hours.

He came back early to discover them unloading guillotines! Others relate a similar account. John saw those who were beheaded for Christ, Revelation 20:4.

The following reasons suggest that trouble may not wait till a Sunday law (3rd angel's message).

1. There were seven 'when-then' signs in 2015. We saw four signs above that were like Cestius coming to Jerusalem before Titus brought death.

2. The 1st angel proclaims a time of judgment. Daniel means God is my Judge and He delivered Daniel from life or death situations in Daniel 1-6; similar for us?

3. The cry at midnight in Matthew 25:6 is an echo of the cry at midnight in Egypt when death fell at Passover. Ellen White likens that cry to "*a sudden unlooked-for calamity*; something that brings the soul face to face with death." COL 412

SDAs think she meant a Sunday law, but that will not come suddenly (GC 606) and SDAs look for it as a sign of end-times. They don't see the 1st angel, a time of judgment, coming first.

But not as the Investigative Judgment since 1844. It's the execution of judgment as in Egypt. God said, "I will execute judgment" Exodus 12:12.

Egypt killed babies, Exodus 1. The US has aborted ~70 million, and the Adventist Health System is guilty as it continues abortions in spite of protest!

"Shall we wait until <u>God's judgments fall</u> upon the transgressor before we tell him how to avoid them? Where is our faith in the word of God?" <u>9T 20</u> That is *not* the "Investigative Judgment." God won't do anything without revealing it, Amos 3:7, but we're not looking!

In the next verse, Amos 3:8, Christ is the Lion of Judah (Rev 5:5) that 'roars'--"The Lord shall roar…<u>the earth shall shake,</u>" Joel 3:16.

This is about a huge earthquake that initiates the end-time *day of the Lord*' in Joel 2:10,11; also in 1Thessalonians 5:2,3 with "sudden destruction."

Christians say "Judgment must begin at the house of God," 1Peter 4:17. In a general way, that's US. In a specific way, it's Adventism that Ellen White saw in vision on a visit to Loma Linda…

"Buildings, great and small, were falling to the ground…Many lives were blotted out…It seemed that Judgment day had come." <u>9T 93</u>

It would help most Adventists to understand the history of Loma Linda. Ellen White said God showed her the property to purchase, but when the day came for the $5000 deposit, church leaders had no money.

They met to discuss what to do when mail came with a check from Mrs. White for $5000!

Loma Linda was to be her school to teach medical missionaries with natural remedies. They could go house-to-house singing gospel songs, giving Bible readings and simple remedies and instruction in health cooking, and praying for the sick.

Had leaders only done as she said, Adventism would have a huge advantage now.

My father, a graduate of the College of Medical Evangelists, told me ~1955, that 85% of his patients would get well, no matter what he did. 10% he helped, 5% would die no matter what he did.

If we applied those figures to what Ellen White wanted, 95% would be well with natural remedies and have no need to get drug prescriptions every month--that is bondage.

There's a crisis in what we call healthcare because the prescription does not usually address the cause and the adverse side effects will sooner or later mean double trouble. Medical care is bondage!

Adventist institutions were to reform the medical practices of the world by their success.

An Impressive Dream

Ellen White described an impressive ship that looked good, but was a "spurious vessel" with worm-eaten timbers that would strike the rocks before reaching harbor in 5T.

What vessel is it that is spurious? In Series B, #7, we read, "All this higher education that is being planned will be extinguished, for it is spurious."

And Kellogg was putting worm-eaten timbers into the medical work. It seems that the dream is about our institutions that aren't doing as she counseled.

The question should somehow dawn on us, at what point do we get off the ship? God in His mercy gave us the answer. It's embedded in the message that Christ said to give again!

"The Bridegroom comes!" We somehow think it's about the 2nd coming and we fail to see the rest of that message--"go ye OUT to meet Him."

SDAs should be ready to leave church fellowship when God's judgment on Loma Linda signals that "Babylon is fallen." (2nd angel's message) If we fail to do so, we may face death as per this video. Here's source, http://drc.whiteestate.org/files/4547.pdf

"How is the faithful city become an harlot?"

Those words from 1903 beg an understanding of history that few SDAs know. When a message of Righteousness by Faith was given in 1888, Ellen White went to campmeetings with Elders Jones and Waggoner to promote the message of righteousness by faith that might be summarized by *Steps to Christ,* but there was more.

When church leaders rejected the message, they asked Ellen White to go to Australia to break up her influence for the 1888 message. She complied but said she could no longer consider the voice of a few men as the voice of God, 9Testimonies, 261

In 1901 she returned to appeal for a re-organization of the General Conference. She didn't want a hierarchical structure, but in 1903, SDA leaders voted it anyway. PT Magan warned them that it was the history of how the Catholic Church formed.

Ellen White's response was, "How is the faithful city become an harlot? My Father's house is made a house of merchandise, a place whence the divine presence and glory have departed," 8T 250

Two years later Ellen White said the apostasy will continue till the Lord comes. *Special Testimonies, Series B, #7*

BT Anderson, retired GC custodian said Series B was burned in the GC furnace--they said the books were extra, not needed.

This fulfills Mrs. White's warning that the burning of Jeremiah's scroll (Jeremiah 36) was history that would be repeated. 4BC 1159.

'For Three Transgressions and for Four' Amos 2

When God said He would not turn away the punishment of Israel's enemies for three or four transgressions, they cheered in Amos 1, but He said so for Israel in chapter 2; it includes us.

Ellen White said we are repeating Israel's history. 1SM 406.

#1. Zechariah 5 shows a woman (church) who is labeled "wickedness" in verse 8, and she is carried to the plain of Shinar (Tower of Babel) by two women with the wings of a stork. Storks are very protective of their young--they are a symbol for maternity wards. In Zech 5, two women (churches) take another church [SDA] to Shinar. It seems that SDA hospitals in NAD do abortions. Zech 5 offers a destiny in Shinar that the NAD doesn't see.

#2. Shinar is where they wanted to "make a name for themselves (Gen 11:4). Under Neal Wilson, the church trademarked the name SDA so nobody can use 'Seventh-day Adventist' without potential lawsuit if the GC chooses. Chick McGill returned from Africa for trial and he went to prison for using the name, 'Creation Seventh-day Adventist Church' in a small Tennessee church.

#3. Trademarking the name after incorporating as a 501 c3 tax-exempt organization has hung us. In this video link, https://www.youtube.com/watch?v=vXHigLTOEbs the church is now compelled to allow homosexuals to hold church office without any discrimination, or it loses its tax-exempt status and

is subject to taxes owed, he says back to when they trademarked the name in the early 1980's--serious errors under Neal Wilson.

Dr. Mervyn Hardinge retired from being the GC Medical Director in 1985 and told this author that "the church is in a state of deep apostasy." It's so from Ellen White's time, 5T 217.

Punishment is coming and it will seem to many SDAs, like the five women who couldn't get into the wedding, that they are robbed of their destiny, but they failed to 'prophesy again' with understanding as we have considered Christ's words. Rev 10:11

Doing so means giving the same messages of 1844 but with better understanding, "when you see Jerusalem compassed with armies" (Lk 21:20) because "Jerusalem is a representation of what the church will be if it refuses to walk in the light," 8T 67.

Ellen White later said we weren't walking in the light, meaning that we would be like Jerusalem—so when we see it compassed with armies, it's about Adventism—"prophesy again!"

Further support for this is Christ's Sermon on the Mount when Christ said, "many will say, Lord, Lord, have we not prophesied in thy name? and in thy name have cast out devils and in thy name done many works?

"Then will I [say] unto them, I never knew you: depart from me…" Matthew 7:22,23. What did He mean--"I never knew you"?

The Greek word _ginosko_ means knowing as in a covenant or marriage--Joseph didn't _know_ Mary till after the child was born. God made a covenant with Israel to prove what was in their heart and He regarded it as marriage--He said, "Return, I am married to you," Jeremiah 3:14.

God is going to give an opportunity for a covenant relationship to be His kingdom and bride as Israel was in Exodus 19:5,6 when they said yes.

But God got an ignorant bride that worshipped a calf 40 days later. This must not happen to Christ.

Embedded in the wedding parables is a provision for Christ to get a wise bride that understands what God wants from us in a pre-nuptial agreement. It's like a wedding feast of betrothal that fits imagery of Passover. Adventists don't do Passover, but we should hear Ellen White on this…

"The Lord Jesus was the foundation of the whole Jewish economy. Its imposing services were of divine appointment. They were designed to teach the people that at the time appointed One would come to whom those ceremonies pointed." COL 34

This includes Christ's coming as a thief if we don't watch-- remember the word means to be awake at Passover when the imagery of Luke 12:37 fits.

"As He ate the Passover with His disciples, He instituted in its place the service that was to be the memorial of His great sacrifice." DA 652.2

"In its place" means on the eve of Passover and if we did so, and then spend some time as Christ said, to 'watch and pray', we would be ready!

That night was a microcosm of end-time events and we don't have to kill lambs or eat bitter herbs, but reviewing the closing scenes of Christ's life as in *Desire of Ages,* is like eating Lamb spiritually, to consider all that He bore for us…

This service was not intended to be weekly as the Catholics do the wafer or quarterly as SDAs have the Lord's Supper.

"The Lord Jesus was the foundation of the whole Jewish economy. Its imposing services were of divine appointment.

They were designed to teach the people that at the time appointed One would come to whom those ceremonies pointed." COL 34

Watching at this time is the only way to be ready--"The types that relate to the second advent must be fulfilled at the time pointed out in the symbolic service." GC 399.4

We are to be ready that "when He comes and knocks, we may open unto Him immediately. Blessed is that servant whom his lord finds watching. He will gird Himself and make him sit down to eat and will come forth and serve him," Luke 12:36,37. And for the servant "so doing…He will make him ruler over all that He has," vs 44. If we don't, we will be "beaten with stripes," vs 47 as end-times begin suddenly for SDAs, COL 412.

The "knock" is an earthquake because the only other place where Christ knocks is in Revelation 3:20, for a lukewarm church that ended in an earthquake circa 63 AD. Are we lukewarm?

America's Christianity is easily that way, and Elder Folkenberg, General Conference President in the 1990's said we are the Laodicean Church.

"So teach us to number our days, that we may apply our hearts unto wisdom." Psalm 90:12

Richard Ruhling, MD, MPH

About the Author

Dr. Richard Ruhling is a retired physician who was board-certified in Internal Medicine and taught Health Science at Loma Linda University and did Executive Health.

He attended cardiology meetings and was influenced by studies that showed heart disease could be reversed by diet. He authored *Why You Shouldn't Ask Your Doctor,* and readers can get a pdf copy free at http://RichardRuhling.com

Since attending a prophecy conference 30+ years ago, end-time topics have been a special interest and the imagery of Christ outside knocking on the church door seems a reality.

Dr. Ruhling is available for speaking on health or Bible. Here's a half-page flyer for local paper or inviting neighbors. You may contact him by email, Ruhling7@juno.com

Add a Decade of Life with a NEW START --
Healthy Habits!

Dr. Breslow of UCLA found 6 or 7 health habits gave an 11-yr advantage over people with 3 or less. Loma Linda University also had a federally-funded study to learn why that community had a similar life advantage.

"While exercise and sleep are important, what we put in our mouths is more critical," says Dr. Richard Ruhling, a physician who taught Health Science at Loma Linda--science supports the things that help to prevent disease also help the body to reverse the disease process.

"We start dying from birth--we can slow up the process if we know how. Our choice of foods determines if we starve ourselves with fad diets that still leave us fat and hungry until we go off the diet, or we can eat all we like and weigh less."

 The seminar designed by Dr. Richard Ruhling, board-certified in Internal Medicine, teaches that people can live better without prescription drugs that have adverse effects--3500 pages in the *Physician's Desk Reference* that he can't remember. We can do our own healthcare with good habits!

Readers may attend a NEW START Seminar that offers triple benefit for $10 registration. ($15 for couples) That includes a low cholesterol buffet meal and the 'Eating' dvd showing how to reverse most diseases by eating. Attendees will see Dr. Esselstyn (Cleveland Clinic cardiologist) and how a diseased artery after heart attack can be healed by changing the diet.

For questions or to register for seating, call (local ABC # to take visa)

*This news release for paper can double as a flyer to invite our neighbors.

Thank you!

Other Websites that may be of interest

http://TheBridegroomComes.com

http://ChooseABetterDestiny.com

http://News4Living.wordpress.com

http://IslamUSinProphecy.wordpress.com

http://TheBridegroomComes.wordpress.com

http://LeadingCauseOfDeathPrescriptionDrugs.com
If you take prescriptions, please visit this site!